Presented to: _____

From: _____

Your word, O LORD, is eternal;
it stands firm in the heavens.

PSALM 119:89

Bible Promises for Women
Copyright ©1998 by the Zondervan Corporation
ISBN: 0-310-97692-8

Excerpts taken from: Women's Devotional Bible: New International Version
Copyright 1990 The Zondervan Corporation All rights reserved.

The Holy Bible: New International Version Copyright 1973, 1978, 1984 by International Bible Society

"NIV" and "New International Version" trademarks are registered in the United States Patent and Trademark Office by International Bible Society.

Requests for information should be addressed to:

ZondervanPublishingHouse
Mail Drop B20
Grand Rapids, Michigan 49530
http://www.zondervan.com

Compiler: Candy Paull
Project Editor: Gwen Ellis

Printed in the United States of America
98 99 00 01 /DP/ 8 7 6 5 4 3 2 1

Give thanks in all circumstances, for this is God's will for you in Christ Jesus.

1 THESSALONIANS 5:18

When your soul feels like a gray February day, and all seems to be rain, fog and chill drizzle, the overcast can be lifted if you will learn to just "keepin' talkin'" with God.

—*Karen Burton Mains*

*I rejoice greatly in the Lord that
at last you have renewed your concern for me.
Indeed, you have been concerned, but
you had no opportunity to show it.*

PHILIPPIANS 4:10

O what a happy soul am I! Although I cannot see, I am resolved that in this world contented I will be; How many blessings I enjoy that other people don't! To weep and sigh because I'm blind, I cannot, and I won't.

—*Fanny Crosby*

$\mathcal{I}$ look back on this day with its usual ups and downs. Its moments of anguish, its moments of gratefulness and joy. For it's been filled with life. The life you have given me to cope with, and to contribute to. And I wouldn't want to have missed it, not a single moment of it.

—*Marjorie Holmes*

Let us hold unswervingly to the hope we profess, for he who promised is faithful.

❦

HEBREWS 10:23

Cultivate a continuous habit of believing, and sooner or later all of your doubts will vanish in the glory of the absolute faithfulness of God.

—*Hannah Whitall Smith*

$\mathcal{S}$mile at someone and find something worth laughing about. As the laughter permeates your life, the spirit of celebration will take root in your heart.

—Emilie Barnes

Go, eat your food with gladness, and drink your wine with a joyful heart, for it is now that God favors what you do.

ECCLESIASTES 9:7

$\mathcal{A}$ joyful heart is the normal result of a heart burning with love. Never let anything so fill you with sorrow as to make you forget the joy of Christ risen.

—*Mother Teresa of Calcutta*

*For you were once darkness,
but now you are light in the Lord.
Live as children of light.*

EPHESIANS 5:8

So God created man in his own image, in the image of God he created him; male and female he created them.

GENESIS 1:27

God created man—male and female—in his own image. What an awesome reality that is. There I am in the first chapter of the Bible— a woman—distinguished from animals, distinguished from my male counterpart, and literally created in the image of God.

—*Ruth A. Tucker*

Through my parents' reading, I learned to love books; through their humor, I learned to laugh; through their discipline, I learned obedience, respect, and self-control. It was through their faith that my own was born.

—*Grace H. Ketterman, M.D.*

I am overwhelmed with gratitude to God for answering my early prayers. I had no status, no special abilities, no money to contribute. Yet the Creator of the universe entered my little room and communed with me about the difficulties I was experiencing. It was awesome to realize that he loved me just as I was.

—*Shirley Dobson*

Commit to the LORD whatever you do, and your plans will succeed.

PROVERBS 16:3

Surrender your blunders to the Lord.
He can use them to make the pattern
of your life more beautiful.

ঙ্গ৯

—*Corrie ten Boom*

When I am afraid, I
will trust in you.

૪ઌ

PSALM 56:3

*O*bedience issues are related not so much to temptations to yield to evil as they are to struggles to do what I should. Procrastination, over-commitment to activities, and not living my priorities are my battlefields.

—Cynthia Heald

The LORD is my strength and my shield; my heart trusts in him, and I am helped. My heart leaps for joy and I will give thanks to him in song.

PSALM 28:7

$\mathscr{I}$ watch the rising mist that heralds the day, and see by God's strong hand the curtain drawn that through the night has hid the world away. So I one day see death's fingers draw back the curtained gloom that shadows life, and on the darkness of time's deepest night, let in the perfect day—Eternity.

—*Alice Macdonald Kipling*

$\mathcal{W}$e are immensely relieved when we find an honest friend whom we can trust. God can be to us that friend. It is impossible for God to lie. When God makes a promise, you can count on him to keep it!

—*Neva Coyle*

Because he himself suffered when he was tempted, he is able to help those who are being tempted.

HEBREWS 2:18

$\mathcal{O}$ur bodies are created with a pace of their own. While disease, heredity, or a physiological breakdown may throw that pace out of whack, more often than not our bodies are responding to the environment we create for them.

—*Barbara DeGroot-Sorensen & David Allen Sorensen*

et the news of him [Jesus] spread all the more, so that crowds of people came to hear him and to be healed of their sicknesses. But Jesus often withdrew to lonely places and prayed.

༄

LUKE 5:16

*J*ust because he has created us as unique individuals, our Father knows the best way to fill each one's empty places. It is only God who can fill our deepest longings.

—*Gini Andrews*

There is a time for everything, and a season for every activity under heaven.

ECCLESIASTES 3:1

"My sheep listen to my voice; I know them, and they follow me. I give them eternal life, and they shall never perish; no one can snatch them out of my hand."

JOHN 10: 27, 28

To sit still . . . for me, that's the posture of Mary—the still prayer of waiting that transforms us in unseen ways.

—Sue Monk Kidd

The areas of my life that I feel are barren, useless, dead, burnt-out—those are the areas that he will fill with nothing less than himself so that I too can be the fullness of him who fills everything in every way.

—*Debby Boone*

$\mathcal{A}$s God showers us with comfort through his Word and through other believers, we in turn are to redirect the stream of his mercy to others. We are not to hoard God's love, but to overflow with the good news of his compassion to all.

—*Barbara Bush*

Give thanks to the LORD, for he is good; his love endures forever.

PSALM 107:1

As we live, work, and bear our burdens, be assured that the melody of our lives is controlled by the eternal God of the universe who knows us from beginning to end.

—*Luci Swindoll*

$\mathcal{G}$od is calling each of us to a life of adventure. Remember, an adventure is not an adventure unless there is some risk involved.

—*Hope MacDonald*

"*Because* you have seen me [Jesus]
you have believed. Blessed are those who
have not seen and yet have believed."

JOHN 20:29

The heart of faith is trusting in the unseen. We have to leap the chasm between that which we know absolutely and that which calls us from within. Even in our uncertainty, we walk in the presence of the holy.

—*Debra Klingsporn*

We do not know what we ought to pray for, but the Spirit himself intercedes for us with groans that words cannot express. And he who searches our heart knows the mind of the Spirit, because the Spirit intercedes for the saints in accordance with God's will.

ROMANS 8:26–27

$\mathcal{T}$he voice of God is always speaking to us, and always trying to get our attention. But his voice is a "still, small voice," and we must at least slow down in order to listen.

ℰ𝒶

—*Eugenia Price*

*J*esus gained new strength when he retreated to commune with his Father. "Come apart with me," Jesus urged his disciples. I need to respond to Jesus' invitation, too.

—Nellie C. Savicki

They shall mount up with wings as eagles; they shall run, and not be weary.

ISAIAH 40:31 (KJV)

*O*ur souls were made to "mount up with wings," and they can never be satisfied with anything short of flying.

❦

—*Hannah Whithall Smith*

*H*ow much is real success dependent on *faithfulness* to what one is doing? It's my thinking that God places no premium on mediocrity.

—*Jeanette Lockerbie*

"*Well done, my good servant!*" *his master replied. "Because you have been trustworthy in a very small matter, take charge of ten cities.*"

LUKE 19:17

I will repay you for the years the locusts have eaten. . . and you will praise the name of the LORD your God.

JOEL 2:25, 26b

It is good to regret missed opportunities, but quite wrong to be miserable about them. Lord Jesus, I give my "if onlies" to you. Make me a faithful laborer here and now.

—*Corrie ten Boom*

By day the LORD directs his love,
at night his song is with me—*a prayer*
to the God of my life.

♫

PSALM 42:8

As we open our hearts and attitudes to God, putting him first in our lives and looking to him for guidance, he will show us little ways to organize our chaos and lead a more peaceful, ordered existence.

—Emilie Barnes

Celebration shows itself in little moments of grace as well as in rambunctious revelry.

—*Emilie Barnes*

Crisis, change. They aren't voices simply of pain but also of creativity. If we would only listen, we might hear such times beckoning us to a season of waiting.

—*Sue Monk Kidd*

God is far more interested in our honesty
than our piety. We have only to offer
him a willing heart and truthful spirit and
he'll take it from there.

—Debra Klingsporn

Offer your bodies as living sacrifices, holy and pleasing to God—this is your spiritual act of worship. Do not conform any longer to the pattern of this world, but be transformed by the renewing of your mind. Then you will be able to test and approve what God's will is—his good, pleasing and perfect will.

ROMANS 12:1-2

$\mathcal{I}$f our lives demonstrate that we are peaceful, humble and trusted, this is recognized by others. If our lives demonstrate something else, that will be noticed too.

—*Rosa Parks*

$\mathcal{Y}$ou don't have to go overseas to be a missionary. You just go into your world and do your best to make a difference. Do what you can one life at a time, right here at home.

—*Babbie Mason*

"For even the Son of Man did not come
to be served, but to serve, and to give
his life as a ransom for many."

MARK 10:45

In a day when servanthood is dying for lack of examples and we get all tied up in theological knots over even the meaning of the word, we might do well to start where Jesus did—with a simple question, "What can I do for you?"

—*Ruth Senter*

His compassions never fail.
They are new every morning;
great is your faithfulness.

❧

LAMENTATIONS 3:22-23

A new day brings with it another opportunity to start all over, to raise one's head from the pillow with a glad heart, to watch the clouds roll across the dark sky now diffusing pink, and to breathe that child prayer of gratitude, "Oh, God, life again. Again, one more day of life."

—*Karen Burton Mains*

$\mathcal{G}$race gives without the receiver realizing how great the gift really is.

—*Rebecca Manley Pippert*

To speak the truth in such a way that it is accepted as something which adds beauty to life, is a great gift.

—*Jean Shaw*

Now *may the Lord of peace himself*
give you peace at all times and in every way.
The Lord be with all of you.

2 THESSALONIANS 3:16

Peace is a gift. God is its guarantee. Whether we personally enjoy this peace is entirely in our own hands. God extends the offer. The acceptance depends on us.

—*Gien Karssen*

There will be a time for every activity, a time for every deed.

ECCLESIASTES 3:17

There's a mystique about timing. When it's right, it's fabulous. When it's wrong, it's a disaster. It takes listening to the inner self to make it work. Not just in comedy, but in all of life.

—*Judith Couchman*

ᴀll of you agree with one another so that there may be no divisions among you and that you may be perfectly united in mind and thought.

1 Corinthians 1:10

*W*hen different races come together,
the worship experience takes on a whole
new dimension. That's what I call the body
of Christ personified.

❦

—*Babbie Mason*

Thank God daily for the precious gift of life. Genuine gratitude and discontent are never found together.

—*Barbara Johnson*

Give thanks to the LORD, for he is good; his love endures forever.

PSALM 107:1

Be still, and know that I am God.
I will be exalted among the nations,
I will be exalted in the earth.

❧

PSALM 46:10

$\mathcal{S}$ilence is full and rich, insistent . . . demanding that I listen and suggesting always that I'd be foolish not to. *Father, teach us to be silent that we might hear your heartbeat in the midst of a noisy world. Amen.*

—*Gloria Gaither & Shirley Dobson*

Lord, when my soul is weary and my heart is tired and sore, and I have that failing feeling that I can't take it any more; then let me know the freshening found in simple, childlike prayer, when the kneeling soul knows surely that a listening Lord is there.

—*Ruth Bell Graham*

$\mathcal{G}$od whispers and we know
that we are safe, because none of us
are ever without help.

—*Brenda Wilbee*

The LORD is near to all who call on him, to all who call on him in truth.

PSALM 145:18

*L*et go completely. Trust. Live with it all in an open hand before God. Jesus promises he will work it all out. I do believe for you, always a new sunrise.

—*Ann Kiemel Anderson*

Jesus promises that satisfaction will come to those who seek the good things of God. He says that they will be filled—not with material goods of this world, not with an easy way of life, . . . but with the joy and contentment that come from doing God's will.

—Colleen Townsend Evans

When one's mind is made up,
this diminishes fear; knowing what
must be done does away with fear.

—Rosa Parks

Do not withhold good from those who deserve it, when it is in your power to act.

PROVERBS 3:27

There are times when you might see a situation that could use something—time, money, skills—that you possess and could share. Don't miss the opportunity to give to someone else.

—*Bernie Sheahan*

*T*here are no doubt many who have illuminated our paths through this life. As we are obedient to his command there will be those whose lives we may brighten. Let your light so shine!

—*Charlotte Stemple*

"*In the same way, let your light shine before men, that they may see your good deeds and praise your Father in heaven.*"

MATTHEW 5:16

The problems we encounter that no one else seems to understand—God sees. The pain we feel—God sees. The tasks we perform for which no one thanks us or pats us on the back—God sees.

—*Mary Maxwell Loeks*

"*Whatever you did for one of the least of these brothers of mine, you did for me.*"

MATTHEW 25:40

*A*ll of life's activities come under his domain. Everything you do can be a way of worshiping the Lord. Remember that, the next time you wash dishes.

—Joni Eareckson Tada

Celebration shines in quiet gratitude that God has blessed our homes and our lives with the spirit of loveliness. We celebrate because our lives overflow with things to be thankful for because God gives us the eyes to see how incredibly we have been blessed.

—*Emilie Barnes*

As far as the east is from the west, so far has he removed our transgressions from us.

❧

PSALM 103:12

When the Lord takes your sins, you never see them again. I even believe that he places a sign over them that reads *No fishing allowed.*

—*Corrie ten Boom*

He has showed you, O man, what is good.
And what does the LORD require of you?
To act justly and to love mercy and to walk
humbly with your God.

MICAH 6:8

$\mathcal{A}$s a friend, I can't heal or change a painful situation. But I can listen with ears that open into my heart.

—Carol Kuykendall

The King will reply, "I tell you the truth, whatever you did for one of the least of these brothers of mine, you did for me."

MATTHEW 25:40

Close your eyes and see yourself as a child in the arms of Jesus. In reassuring words he speaks to you: "My child, I care about you. I love you unconditionally. Trust me. I love you."

—Rosalind Rinker

The great artists keep us from frozenness, from smugness, from thinking that the truth is in us, rather than in God, in Christ our Lord. They help us to know that we are often closer to God in our doubts than in our certainties.

—*Madeleine L'Engle*

But [the Lord] *said to me, "My grace is sufficient for you, my power is made perfect in weakness." Therefore I will boast all the more gladly about my weaknesses, so that Christ's power may rest on me.*

2 CORINTHIANS 12:9

The resurrection of Christ brought love among us, and it is the very principle of our existence. If we recognize this, we can transform the world.

—*Catherine Doherty*

Have I not commanded you? Be strong and courageous. Do not be terrified; do not be discouraged, for the LORD your God will be with you wherever you go.

JOSHUA 1:9

Jesus answered: "Love the Lord your God with all your heart and with all your soul and with all your strength and with all your mind"; and, "Love your neighbor as yourself."

LUKE 10:27

Today a great disease is that feeling of terrible loneliness, the feeling of being unwanted, having forgotten what human joy is, what the human feeling is of being wanted or loved.

—*Mother Teresa of Calcutta*

Many are the plans in a man's heart, but it is the LORD's purpose that prevails.

PROVERBS 19:21

$\mathcal{W}$e may not be able to march into a foreign country and bring oppressors to justice. But we can pray. Through our prayers, God changes situations that baffle even the most skilled negotiators.

—*Edith Bajema*

I pray that you may be active in sharing your faith, so that you will have a full understanding of every good thing we have in Christ.

PHILEMON 6-7

$\mathcal{M}$y moments of being most complete, most integrated, have come either in complete solitude or when I am being part of a body made up of many people going in the same direction.

—*Madeleine L'Engle*

*B*lessed is the man who perseveres under trial, because when he has stood the test, he will receive the crown of life that God has promised to those who love him.

JAMES 1:12

The most difficult thing to let go is my self, that self which, coddled and cozened, becomes smaller as it becomes heavier. I don't understand how and why I come to be only as I lost myself, but I know from long experience that this is so.

—Madeleine L'Engle

I pray that out of his glorious riches he may strengthen you with power through his Spirit in your inner being.

EPHESIANS 3:16

*L*ord, sometimes I feel happy, sometimes I feel sad, hurt, and disappointed. Thank you for not rejecting me because I feel.

—*Joan Webb*

Arise, shine, for your light is come, and the glory of the LORD rises upon you. See, darkness covers the earth and thick darkness is over the peoples, but the LORD rises upon you and his glory appears over you.

ISAIAH 60:1-2

$\mathcal{E}$xposing ourselves to the light and presence of the Lord's love not only will uncover the dark places of our hearts but also will fill them with light.

—*Debby Boone*

But the fruit of the Spirit is love, joy, peace, patience, kindness, goodness, faithfulness.

GALATIANS 5:22

$\mathcal{J}$oy is a net of love by which
you can catch souls.

$\mathcal{S}$

—*Mother Teresa of Calcutta*

I praise you because I am fearfully and wonderfully made; your works are wonderful, I know that full well.

PSALM 139:14

$\mathcal{G}$od loves each one of us as though there were only one of us to love. Because of it, we can live in the certainty that his grace is sufficient for us today, regardless of our circumstances.

—Hope MacDonald

God is a God of abundance, even a God of excess. He doesn't do things halfway.

❧

—*Anne Christian Buchanan*

"As the rain and the snow come down from heaven, and do not return to it without watering the earth and making it bud and flourish . . . so is my word that goes out from my mouth: It will not return to me empty, but will accomplish what I desire and achieve that purpose for which I sent it."

ISAIAH 55:10-11

And we know that in all things God works for the good of those who love him, who have been called according to his purpose.

ROMANS 8:28

$\mathcal{G}$od created us in order to love us and taste our love, to delight in us and enjoy our delight. God wants our hearts.

—*Sue Monk Kidd*

The hard thing to understand is that faith is the one area in our lives where growing up means we must grow to be more like a child, trusting simply in the goodness and complete knowledge of a Father who has our best interests at heart.

—*Colleen Townsend Evans*

And without faith it is impossible to please God, because anyone who comes to him must believe that he exists and that he rewards those who earnestly seek him.

HEBREWS 11:6

In moments when you are touched by the soul of a child, you suddenly realize the eternal significance of these precious years. Then, no other task on earth seems quite as important or meaningful as raising and training and guiding through developmental experiences.

—*Shirley Dobson*

May your father and mother be glad; may she who gave you birth rejoice!

PROVERBS 23:25

For if you forgive men when they sin against you, your heavenly Father will also forgive you.

MATTHEW 6:14

When we forgive, we open
a channel to God.

✌

—Hope MacDonald

"*Let the little children come to me,
and do not hinder them.*"

∂∽

MATTHEW 19:14

*H*ospitality toward children is not simply a matter of being open toward our own, but it requires that we accept, encourage and want those born of someone else whether we have children of our own or not.

—Karen Burton Mains

*For you were once darkness,
but now you are light in the Lord.
Live as children of light.*

❦

EPHESIANS 5:8

$\mathscr{L}$et's pursue that which is good, right and truthful by shining through darkened circumstances. Don't keep the switch off or hold back as though our batteries have run down. Being switched on pleased the Lord. Stay on. Stay bright.

—Luci Swindoll

$\mathcal{L}$et God's big hand close gently over yours. With his help, even the discouraging scribbles of your life can become a masterpiece. Nothing would delight a father's heart more.

—*Joni Eareckson Tada*

We proclaim to you what we have seen and heard, so that you also may have fellowship with us. And our fellowship is with the Father and with his Son, Jesus Christ. We write this to make our joy complete.

1 JOHN 1:3-4

But those who hope in the LORD will renew their strength. They will soar on wings like eagles; they will run and not grow weary, they will walk and not be faint.

ISAIAH 40:31

*W*hen I come to the end of myself, wherever I am in the world, God is there. And from that seeming dead end He can create new life, and give new strength. I never need fear that I have not taken him along.

※

—*Gladis and Gordon DePree*

"*For I know the plans I have for you,*" declares the LORD, "*plans to prosper you and not to harm you, plans to give you hope and a future.*"

JEREMIAH 29:11

$\mathcal{W}$e don't have to settle for blandness in life; God, who is the Author of creativity, is ready to make a dull life adventuresome the moment we allow his Holy Spirit to go to work inside us.

—*Catherine Marshall*

The LORD your God is with you, he is mighty to save. He will take great delight in you.

ZEPHANIAH 3:17

I need to stop, close my eyes and see myself as I really am—God's child, tucked safely inside his care, incredibly privileged, and utterly surrounded by beautiful, golden light.

❦

—*Anne Christian Buchanan*

In everything I did, I showed you that by this kind of hard work we must help the weak, remembering the words the Lord Jesus himself said: "It is more blessed to give than to receive."

ACTS 20:35

$\mathcal{I}$f you seek to be understood, then dedicate your life to understanding others. If you seek to be comforted, then dedicate yourself to giving comfort. If you seek a greater faith, then commit yourself to planting it in others.

—*Sue Monk Kidd*

And God is able to make all grace abound to you, so that in all things at all times, having all that you need, you will abound in every good work.

இ

2 CORINTHIANS 9:8

When we become absorbed in something demanding and worthwhile above and beyond ourselves, happiness seems to be there as a by-product of the self-giving.

—Catherine Marshall

He calls his own sheep by name
and leads them out.

JOHN 10:3

Jesus calls to you in the night, as you lie down to sleep. He calls to you in the morning when you awake. Let yourself hear him. Listen for the voice of the Good Shepherd, calling you by name.

—*Edith Bajema*

Celebrating each new day helps us develop the ability to be grateful for all new moments and for the God who is in each one. The discipline of celebrating each new day influences our attitude toward all of life.

—*Karen Burton Mains*

Children have a wonderful ability to accept the gifts of God at face value, without feeling pride or embarrassment.

—*Debby Boone*

This poor man called, and the LORD heard him;
he saved him out of all his troubles.

PSALM 34:6

The meaning of my life is the love of God. It is Christ in his distressing disguise whom I love and serve.

—*Mother Teresa of Calcutta*

The earth is the LORD's,
and everything in it.

🙵

PSALM 24:1

*M*oses was informed by God that where he was standing was holy ground. He took off his shoes. To revere the earth and its beauty as the wondrous work of God . . . that's something I can take my shoes off for.

—*Bernie Sheahan*

*Then he calls his friends and neighbors
together and says, "Rejoice with me;
I have found my lost sheep."*

LUKE 15:6

We often shrink from calling anything "sin," but we do admit that sometimes we find ourselves alone, lost, and away from our Shepherd.

—*Rosalind Rinker*

$\mathcal{W}$e must ever be praying—
breathing vertically—if we are to have
any wisdom from above.

🙽

—*Joni Eareckson Tada*

Therefore I tell you, whatever you ask for in prayer, believe that you have received it, and it will be yours.

MARK 11:24

*A generous man will prosper;
he who refreshes others will
himself be refreshed.*

❧

PROVERBS 11:25

$\mathcal{A}$s you refresh others, you relieve your own pain. Try "refreshing or watering" another person's life. You will find that your own pain is lessened.

—*Barbara Johnson*

It's easy to mistake meanness for moderation, stinginess for self-discipline, laziness for maturity, fear for wisdom. *God, only in your love can I learn the balance of choosing wisely but investing myself fully.*

—Anne Christian Buchanan

Serve wholeheartedly, as if you were serving the Lord, not men.

❧

EPHESIANS 6:7

*W*hat I formerly called faith is little better than having invited God into the parlor of my life while I checked his references. God is moving me toward a faith that is wide and free and at ease with uncertainty.

—*Paula Rinehart*